Fearless

A 31 Day Devotional

CRYSTAL JONES

Copyright © 2017 Crystal Jones

All rights reserved.

Destiny House Publishing, LLC

www.destinyhousepublishing.com

email: inquiry@destinyhousepublishing.com

P.O. Box 19774 Detroit, MI 48219

Artwork by Shutterstock and CanStock

Cover by RLSmith Designs

ISBN: 1936867273
ISBN-13: 978-1936867271

DEDICATION

I dedicate this book to the darlings of my heart, my granddaughters: Kristin D'Ashley, Arielle Joy, Kennedy Demara, and Lauren Rachel Ann. You were chosen by God to bless my life and you have in ways that you are not even aware. It is my desire to see you beauties soar through this life, full of courage. In order for that to happen you must first commit to God. Follow Him as He unfolds the amazing plan He has for your life. I pray that you would do the unimaginable, break molds, and be little trailblazers. If I could leave anything to you when I leave the earth, it would be my fearlessness and my devotion to the Lord. I love you with all that I am.

I also dedicate this book to each and every one of my natural sisters: Tina Clark, Kimberly Owens, Joyce Underwood, and Patrice Williams. I love you more than you know. My prayer for you is that you would be fearless and full of faith. Do all that's in your heart to do for God's kingdom. Break out of the ordinary and live the life you were born to lead!

And finally, I dedicate this book to all of God's daughters all over the world. Grow and flourish, and be all that God has called you to be.

CONTENTS

	Acknowledgments	i
	Introduction	1
1	God Loves Me	3
2	Taking God At His Word	7
3	No More Fears	11
4	Waiting to Exhale	15
5	Laugh Out Loud	19
6	Valleys	23
7	Second Guessing	27
8	Hypotheticals	31
9	Speak Up!	35
10	Get A Clue	41
11	The Fight Is Not Over	43
12	Fear Is Sin	47
13	God In Your Equation	51
14	God Is For Us	55
15	People Pleasing	59
16	The Fear of Lack	63
17	Doctor's Report	67
18	Stormy Weather	71

19	Critical Condition	75
20	Broken Love	79
21	Sleep In Heavenly Peace	83
22	Be Still	87
23	He Is With Me	91
24	Good Grief	95
25	Out of Control	99
26	Chameleon	103
27	Shame, Shame, Shame	107
28	God-fidence	111
29	Distractions	115
30	Battle Scars	119
31	Giving Birth	123
	Fearless Prayer	127
	About the Author	129

FEARLESS

Fear never wrote a symphony or a poem,

Negotiated a peace treaty or cured a disease,

Fear never pulled a family out of poverty or a country out of bigotry.

Fear never saved a marriage or a business.

Courage did that.

Faith did that.

People who refused to consult or cower to their timidities did that.

-Max Luxado in *Fearless*-

ACKNOWLEDGMENTS

Thank you, Lord for continually pouring into me and causing me to shed layers and layers of fear. I am in awe of this whole fearless journey. Thank you for calling me to it. I, wholeheartedly accept the challenge. I will go, do, and be all that you ask.

Thanks to my husband, Oscar Jones, for your patience with my process and your unending love and support. You are the most fearless person I know. Thank you for sharing this life with me.

I also want to thank my amazing Fearless Team: Keila Allen, Hashina Brumfield, Charity Dean, Pam Gary, Candace Graham, Karen Grier, Lakeisha Grier, Kyria Jones, LaTina Jones, Rochelle Smith, Debbie Townley, Yolanda Williams, Aries Winans, and Kim Edwards Winans. You make me better and bring me higher. Thank you for your love and support.

INTRODUCTION

Every person on the earth will have to deal with fear in some way or another. No one is exempt. When it rears its ugly head, that is the time to face fear head on. Identify the source of your fear. Confess your fear to God. Then turn to your fear and faith it. To faith it is to boldly confront it. Don't meditate on it or magnify it, but speak the Word and move forward in action.

Fear often comes in layers. We, sometimes, don't even realize that what we are feeling is fear because fear tends to camouflage itself. If we don't recognize it, we will allow it to remain. And if it remains, it can paralyze us and cause us to abort the destiny that God has in store.

So I challenge you to this 31 day study to eradicate fear in your life. Go all the way through to the end. Study the scriptures associated with each daily thought. Meditate on the verse and pray over it.

As you proceed in this devotional, be open to see fear in ways you may not have imagined. Don't draw back. It's only when you see fear, that you can defeat it. So be transparent with yourself.

It is not necessary to go in any particular order. Each study can stand on its own. So go in any order you choose. Just make sure you complete each one.

Write In The Sand

is the section where you ponder the daily scripture you read and answer questions as they pertain to you. Be thorough and honest with yourself. It's for your eyes only. See this devotion time as your intimate one and one time with the Lord.

Go Fearless

is the challenge for the day. There will be some action that you will be asked to take. Don't skip over this part. It is key to stepping out of your fear and walking out the bold, adventurous life to which you have been called. Take the leap. Minimize your fear by doing it afraid. You will maximize your faith...and soar!

DAY 1

GOD LOVES ME

There is no fear in love. But perfect love drives out fear, because fear has to do with torment. The one who fears is not made perfect in love.
I John 4:18 NIV

Perfect love means we love and trust God completely and fully. Our hearts are filled with love for the God that loved us first It is the ultimate love – defined by sacrifice. We love Him so much that we willingly lay down our lives for Him. Because indeed, isn't that how He demonstrated his love for us? When our hearts are filled with love for our God, there is NO room for anything else. Doubt, unbelief, anxiety are all diminished by love.

Love produces a God confidence that makes us unshakable. Perfect love has no worry that God won't come through. We trust Him and take Him at His word. It is having the ability to free fall into his arms knowing He will catch us. Our expectation is that He will do exactly what He says He will do. We don't expect him to fail us or ignore us. We don't hold back in our relationship for fear of disappointment. Our confidence in His love pushes us forward in faith. He is worthy of our trust.

Our God's love must become more than a biblical truth. It must be how we live. As His love is revealed to us we become more and more confident. It is our way of life – loving God and being loved by Him.

Initially this love is difficult to grasp because men do not naturally love like this. But God loves us in spite of ourselves. So He will come through. He will not allow His word to fall to the ground. He has a track record of giving us more than we deserve.

He loves us even more than we venture to love ourselves. And He cares about everything that concerns us, even if we think it's too small for God's attention. God will speak to it. He means us good and not evil.

His love is not based upon our action or inaction. It is not defined by our human efforts. He loves simply because He is love. We can't earn it or lose it. The amazing love of our God is generous and lavish. He wants us to accept it, bask in it, and be filled with it.

If we can grow to receive a love like this, that creates a Fearless life.

WRITE IN THE SAND:

What holds you back in your love relationship with God?

_____

_____

_____

_____

What do you fear that God won't do for you? Why?

_____

_____

_____

GO FEARLESS

Think about God's love for you. Create a document and add to it. Record every way that God has expressed His love for you over your entire life. Add to it as things come to mind.

DAY 2

TAKING GOD AT HIS WORD

Fear not, for I am with you; be not dismayed, for I am your God; I will strengthen you, I will help you, I will uphold you with my righteous right hand. Isaiah 41:10 ESV

When trepidation floods our hearts, it's great to hear the words, "Don't fear" or "Don't be afraid". However the words alone are not enough. It's much more important that we turn the focus to the speaker. See it doesn't mean much if the speaker has his own issues and worries. How can one encourage us not to draw back when you too have a host of fears. So who is speaking? Who is offering us such bold words? This is no anonymous philosopher. But these words stem straight from the heart of God.

Before we can accept the promise we must know something of the promise giver. This is the God that laid it all on the line for us. His life for ours. He is our defender and protector and amazing Lover of our souls. He has a history of showing up for us. And the judgment we deserved, he wouldn't let us serve it. He stood in our stead and justified us by our faith in Him. He is the God that shows up and keeps his word. He has shown himself strong on our behalf countless times.

God is not a man that He should lie or the son of man that he should change his mind. Has he said, and will he not do it? Or has he spoken, and will he not fulfill it? Numbers 23:19 He is truth, therefore it is impossible for Him to lie.

He forgives us, loves us, delivers us and heals us. The One who took our punishment. The God who loves us fully and covers us completely. He is the One who issues this promise, **"I am with**

you". That is loaded. He not only tells us not to fear, but he tells us why we need not fear, 'He is with us'. He is on our side. He walks with us through fire and floods. He will not let us be overtaken. He will rush in beside us. And He promises to help us.

He is a personal God. He says I am YOUR God, not THE God or A God. He is speaking to those with whom He has a relationship. Deeper than any relationship of kin is that of one's God. We do not necessarily trust our kin. Nor are we necessarily close. Even when there is a close relationship, it is still nothing compared to that of the God-lover relationship. It's much more intimate. We worship our God. Weaknesses are exposed. Secrets are shared. And His love covers. We submit to him our trust and obeisance.

He extends the promise. I will strengthen you. I will help you. I will uphold you with my righteous right hand.

So He doesn't leave us guessing. Yes, he is with us. But He also lets us know that His presence is not without power. He will act on our behalf. We don't need to send for help. Help is already with us. We cannot be defeated.

So there really is no reason to fear. We have a perpetual promise that God is with us. No matter what we face, we never face it alone. Our God is never absent. He stands by our side ready to hand over the victory to us. He who has helped us before will help us again. That's enough to go on.

WRITE IN THE SAND:

Who is God to you? Write as if you are introducing Him to a friend.

_____

_____

_____

_____

_____

_____

_____

How can you draw closer to God?

_____

_____

_____

GO FEARLESS

Think about the many ways that the Lord has come to your rescue. Pray and identify someone that you can help this week. Let the Lord use you to help a friend, co-worker, or neighbor or even a distant family member.

DAY 3

NO MORE FEARS

I sought the Lord and He answered me and delivered me from all my fears. Psalm 34:4

Can you imagine what it would feel like to go through life without any fear? Never dreading anything? It would be exhilarating. What an enormous freedom you would embody! You would soar through this life doing whatever you felt called to do without any inhibitions. You would be fully operating in purpose.

But isn't this the will of God for His people? God asks us to trust Him. That means submitting every single fear to him. David did it. And the result was that God delivered him from ALL of his fears. What a bold Psalm!

David prayed and God answered him. David assures us that God will answer with deliverance. It is incumbent upon us to seek Him. So what was David's prayer? Was it Lord deliver me from all of this trouble? Not at all. David prayed deliver me from my fears. What a more important prayer! Cause me to consider you and rely on you. All trouble is not bad for us. The trying of our faith works patience in our lives. Trouble brings with it humility, gratitude and compassion. We all can benefit from trouble in this life. But fear in itself serves no good purpose. And David recognized that. What if we ventured toward living the fearless life instead of the trouble-free life?

Fearless living is better than trouble-free living. Fearlessness grants us the privilege of freedom, security, and internal peace. What a life! Think of all the things that you would be able to do if fear was not a factor? Would you find yourself more obedient to

God? Can you imagine being free of intimidation, not worried about people's opinions?

David attained a level of living that most people never even imagine is possible. Yet it is available just for the asking. We are to take those fears to God and empty them at his feet. Seek God for the fear-free life.

In the midst of affliction, we are compelled to run to God just as David did. He was in dire straits. But he asked a more holy petition. The essence of his prayer was, "Lord, don't deliver me from the affliction, but take away the fear that is packaged with it." When fear is absent we can see and hear God more clearly. Our faith is set ablaze. We can stand boldly against the enemy. And we indeed will run through a troop and leap over a wall.

God is calling us to heroism and a life of courage. It is our portion as faithful believers. We can do all things through Christ which strengthens us.

WRITE IN THE SAND:

With what fears are you presently struggling?

_____

_____

What if the fear was removed and the trouble was still present? What would you do differently?

_____

_____

_____

_____

GO FEARLESS

Look at your list of fears. Choose one thing and challenge yourself to do the opposite of the thing you fear. Example: Fear of rejection. Step out of your place of comfort. Look for an opportunity to face rejection (i.e. ask your boss for a raise/promotion, apologize to someone you wronged, etc.)

DAY 4

WAITING TO EXHALE

*They will have no fear of bad news;
their hearts are steadfast, trusting in the LORD..
Psalm 112:7 NIV*

If you've ever been in a position where you were waiting for the other shoe to fall, you understand what it can feel like to expect or anticipate bad news. At some time in your life, you will find yourself waiting; whether it's a court decision, results from a test for cancer, potential job loss, an offer made on a property, a committee appeal, forgiveness from a spouse, etc.

But the righteous do not fear bad news. There is no apprehension about what is to come. Why? Because the righteous trust in God's care. To know Him is to trust Him. So the righteous approach every situation with complete abandonment surrendering their lives into His hands. Waiting is always accompanied with a 'Lord, I trust you'. God means us good and not evil. I know the thoughts I have towards you, of peace and not of evil to give you an hope and a future. Jeremiah 29:11

So even if the results aren't what I expected, I still believe. I can rest in His love. It's His love that will comfort and carry me through tough times. As you meditate on the love of God, fear dissipates. No matter what the news is. At some of the most traumatic times in my life when I have received the most devastating news, those have been the times that I could only utter the words, 'Lord, I trust you.'

Others don't know what the righteous know. You can't fear bad news, for what will it profit you? You pray for God's best and keep on moving. Keep on believing and trust that God has got you. Never allow any type of news to push you off your marker.

You are a believer, therefore you must believe.

Sometimes the path we take is not direct. We must venture around mountains, through caves and down into valleys. But God will get us where we ought to be. He only has good plans and intentions for us. He is not a sinister God plotting and scheming against us. We have but one enemy, Satan. He is the one who brings and promotes evil on the earth. Even so, we don't need to brace ourselves for the worst, tightening our backs as if that will keep it from coming. No, we rest in God's peace. We trust Him for the best. We hope against hope. Yes, sometimes the worst will come. But even if it does, we will get through it because God is on our side. And He insists on caring for us.

His yoke is easy and his burden is light. We are to cast every care on Him. We weren't built to carry our own burdens.

So when news comes. Believe for the good. Don't get all tangled up in worry that it will be bad news. Trust that even in those rare times when it is bad, God will navigate you through it. You may have to take a few detours, but you will still reach your destination.

WRITE IN THE SAND:

Are you waiting for some results or news to come in about a particular situation? What is it? Do you expect it to be negative or positive?

_____

_____

_____

_____

What is the worst thing that could happen? If that worst thing happens, can God handle it? He has handled things like this before?

_____

_____

_____

_____

GO FEARLESS

Sow a financial seed. Be prayerful and ask the Lord to choose the person you are to bless. Once you have identified them, give it anonymously. Let God be glorified. If possible, choose someone who has received bad news lately.

DAY 5

LAUGH OUT LOUD

Strength and dignity are her clothing, and she laughs at the time to come. Proverbs 31:25 KJV

When Sarah was given a promise from God of her future, the Bible says she laughed. God then challenged Abram, "Why did Sara laugh?" Her laugh indicated unbelief. The promise was so far-fetched for Sara. Here she was in her old age, past child-bearing season and it is at this time that she is promised a son. What was God thinking? She mused.

Her whole life she longed for a son. And God waits until she is no longer ripe and says okay, now it's time! Her natural mind could not even fathom such a gift. So she laughed. It wasn't that it was funny to her. I imagine it was a somber laugh, filled with disappointment. Could she dare to believe that this long awaited prophecy would come to pass. Too much time had passed. It was just futile to believe. It hurt her too much to hope. She wanted it to be true. But she had heard this word before and it had not come to pass in all of this time.

But God challenges Sara with these words, "Is anything too hard for God? Things that are impossible with men are possible with God. Whew! He heard the wonderings in her heart. He heard every doubtful thought, every question in her mind. And he addressed it. He never withdrew the promise but he wanted her to understand that her future was not limited to natural circumstances. She was not shackled to only what men could do. But her life was indeed limitless in Him.

However the opening scripture for today speaks of the Virtuous Woman. *She laughs at the time to come..* Her laughter is strong and confident. It is not laced with unbelief. Her laughter denotes trust. The Virtuous Woman is confidently glad about her future. She expects that it is good. Even if the world is in distress and calamity around her, she is yet able to smile at her own future. I imagine she has a secret. Maybe, the Lord has allowed her to peer into her future. Or perhaps she is simply laughing in faith because she knows God so well. He has proven that He can be trusted. Nevertheless, she laughs. With no worries about what's ahead, she triumphantly marches forward.

The book of wisdom says that laughter is good medicine. It's a laughter that has no fear. It's the kind of laughter that floods your heart with joy. Have you ever laughed so hard and intently that it just felt good when it was over? It felt good to your soul. Well God is calling you to laugh. Your future looks good. The thing that He has promised will come to pass. Go ahead, laugh out loud.

WRITE IN THE SAND:

The two women laugh at their futures. Sarah and the Virtuous Woman. What is the sound of your laughter? Are you laughing in doubt or faith? Why?

_____

_____

_____

_____

Is there an old prophecy or promise from God that you have tucked away in disbelief? Maybe you believe it's past its expiration date. Record it here. Pray over it.

_____

_____

_____

_____

_____

_____

_____

GO FEARLESS

Get a visual of your future: Create a vision board or vision book. Cut out pictures from a magazine or print pictures online to create a visual snapshot of your future according to God's plan.

DAY 6

VALLEYS

Yea though I walk through the darkest valley, I will fear no evil, for you are with me. Psalm 23:4 NIV

Broken hearts, death, divorce, unemployment, terminal illness, miscarriages, etc. are all types of valleys. There are dips in life. And this life being what it is, we all must encounter a valley at some point in our lifetime. We can't detour valleys. There is no way to avoid them.

What is our response when we stumble up on one? The psalmist takes a stand. He defies his circumstances, "I won't be afraid!" Even in the darkest time, I refuse to fear. Because just as you promised, Lord, you are with me. Can we make the same type of dogmatic declaration? The season may be dark but I reject fear.

My brother had been shot in the back and was rushed by ambulance to the hospital. My sister called franticly, she believed my brother was already dead. My mom was hysterical after receiving the phone call. I tried to calm her down. "Mom, we don't know anything, yet. Let's just wait to hear." Just as I got her to calm down, the other phone rang. Indeed my baby brother was dead. The shrill of my mother's voice was an anguish that came from her soul. My brother was no longer living and breathing on this earth. He was gone... just like that. Our entire family had plummeted into a valley.

Our ministry was in its infancy, we were barely 2 months old. What would we do? We had never performed a eulogy. How would we comfort so many others when we needed comfort ourselves. This was all a bit much.

One year prior, I had dreamed that my brother was murdered. I shared it with many family members, but I hadn't said anything to him. Would I be consumed with guilt? What was to come?

As we prepared to bury him, a song rung in my spirit, "Jesus, You're The Center of My Joy." I held tightly to his hand. I was so glad to have him close. My heart had been broken. And He was the only One who could console me. Yes, though I walk through the valley of the shadow of death, I won't fear. The promise was that I would get to the other side of this pain. He would not leave me in the middle of it. God comforted us and got us through that dreadful time. We didn't fall apart or lose our minds. We made it securely to the other side. He pulled us up out of that pit.

Understand that we will walk "through" valleys. We will cry, hurt, lose, and suffer. But know that *walking through a valley* signifies victory. It lets us know that the valley experience is temporary. We won't camp out in the valley but we continue moving forward in faith. We keep walking <u>through</u>. We don't sit down in defeat. Fearlessness keeps us forging forward. We are destined to get to the other side. We boldly declare out of our mouths that we won't fear any evil. And then we walk that out. He is in the valley with us nudging us onward. We are confident that the Good Shepherd watches over His Sheep and will not allow them to stay in a pit.

It's appointed unto man once to die and then the judgment. Death is a constant. We will bury others until it's someone's time to bury us. Because of sin, there will be valleys to walk through. The promise is that we won't have to muddle through it alone. God will hold our hand with each step. There is comfort even in the valley.

WRITE IN THE SAND:

Are you in a valley season of your life? If yes, describe it. If no, when was the last time you encountered the valley?

_____

_____

_____

_____

_____

Create a psalm giving praise to God for being with you.

_____

_____

_____

_____

GO FEARLESS

Identify a person in your life who is in a valley. What type of valley are they in? Commit to pray for them every day for 7 days. Send a card of encouragement.

DAY 7

SECOND GUESSING

They had rowed three or four miles when suddenly they saw Jesus walking on the water toward the boat. They were terrified, but he called out to them, "Don't be afraid. I am here!" John 6:19-20 NLT

Have you ever been following the will of God and things seemed to be falling apart? I mean, you were doing exactly as you were instructed and then out of nowhere, here comes one of the biggest storms of your life? Sometimes, the storm is so intense, it makes you second guess, "Did God really tell me to do this?" This is what happened to the disciples. God had told them to go to the other side. They were following his instruction when all hell broke loose. These skilled fishermen could not handle this monster of a storm. And if that didn't beat all, it looked like a ghost was coming toward them.

Fear grabbed them by the throat and seemed to choke the faith right out of them. But at the peak of their fear, the Lord speaks. "Don't be afraid, I am here." Still not completely convinced, Peter asks him to prove it. "Bid me to come." And the Lord concedes. There is so much in this story. The Lord sees them struggling and comes to where they are. He will never leave us or turn his back on us. But just like a loving parent, he rushes in to rescue us.

The promise for us all is that whatever we are going through – it's not what it looks like. It may look like we are doomed. It looks like we won't succeed in doing what God asks of us. It looks like our situation is hopeless and that we are alone. Not so. God is sovereign. And though the storm may surprise you, it never surprises the Lord. He is in complete control. He calmly walks on stormy waves. "It is I", the Lord said. Don't worry about what you think it is. I am in charge. The enemy is in the waves but he is not the One walking on them.

We don't get to escape trouble just because we are believers. Trials and tribulations most certainly will come. We should remember that the enemy of God has become our enemy also. We can follow God's instructions knowing full well Satan will "try" to intimidate us. Nevertheless our hero rushes in – No need to fear. God is here! He will walk on the very thing that has come to shake us. Victory belongs to Jesus and therefore it belongs to us.

WRITE IN THE SAND:

What has God told you told you to do that you are second guessing.

_____

_____

_____

_____

_____

_____

_____

GO FEARLESS

Go on a prayer walk. Identify a nudge in your spirit from God. Something you believe God is telling you to do. Do it today. Do not delay any longer.

DAY 8

HYPOTHETICALS

He said to his disciples, "Why are you so afraid? Do you still have no faith? " St. Mark 4:40 NIV

The disciples were in a state of panic. Jesus was sleeping and their ship was being tossed to and fro by tumultuous winds and waves. In fact, things were so bad, the disciples began to predict what would happen. "We are going to die!" It makes you wonder what was going on in their minds. Did they think that the boat would capsize and they would be swept over into the water or did they think that the water would fill the boat? Either way, they were sure that death was eminent. And so they went to awake Jesus asking him an accusatory and offensive question, "Do you care?" It was an indictment on His character.

Maybe you have found yourself in one of life's many storms. How did you respond? Did you question God's love for you? Or do you rest in His unfailing love?

We sometimes can get caught up in the 'Hypotheticals'. 'Hypotheticals' are not real. They are negative forecasts – worst-case scenarios. They are usually activated by some situation or circumstance and take you down a hopeless road. 'Hypotheticals' can consume you and have you in a state of panic and anxiety over what "could" happen. One thing is sure. If you are entertaining hypotheticals, you are definitely not operating in the realm of faith. And the longer you stay there, the deeper you go. You will find yourself wondering, "Does God really care?"

Maybe you get a phone call from a loved one and the message is cut off. You hear them breathing heavily and they say your name and then the phone goes dead. Do you believe that all is well and you will eventually reach them or do you imagine that someone was after them maybe trying to kill them. If only you had been able to pick up the phone when they called, they might still be alive. Sounds wild? But that's exactly how it happens. When we respond to a single situation without faith, it causes us to exaggerate it. And we imagine the worst. Just like the disciples. They were in a storm. It was not going to kill them and especially not on Jesus's watch.

After Jesus rebuked the winds and the waves, he asked them why were they so afraid? They should not have been. They were born to handle this. Empowered to speak to storms. Jesus had power sure, but they had power also. The fact of the matter is we cannot be in fear and faith at the same time. We must choose to let one or the other occupy our hearts. Which will it be?

Choose to avoid the path of hypotheticals. Believe by faith that it will work out just as God said. Hold on to your faith.

WRITE IN THE SAND:

Do you questioned God's love for you? Why?

_____

_____

_____

Write a situation that is in your life right now. Take it down the road of faith instead of fear. What is the best thing that could possibly happen?

_____

_____

_____

_____

GO FEARLESS:

Identify a scripture on faith to apply to your present situation. Write it down. Memorize it. Post it on your bathroom mirror in your kitchen cabinets. Speak it every time you see it and whenever 'hypotheticals' try to creep in.

DAY 9

SPEAK UP

Pray also for me, that whenever I speak, words may be given me so that I will fearlessly make know the mystery of the gospel. Eph 6:19 NIV

There are hundreds of phobias in the earth. However the number one fear that affects most people is glossophobia, the fear of public speaking. At some point we will be called upon to speak a few words for the cause of Christ. Whether it's in a living room, a classroom, an auditorium or a stadium, we should prepare ourselves.

We worry that we won't have anything to say or that we will say too much. We stress over saying the wrong thing. Or we worry that what we say won't be received. It can be overwhelming. While there has been much written on how to overcome fear of public speaking, Paul goes right for the most effective method – prayer. He asks the church to pray for him. He takes nothing for granted. He doesn't rest on his talent or abilities. Paul enlists the help of others.

We admire those that are able to speak with comfortable confidence. It seems so natural to them. But we don't know is -it is often prayer that has gotten them to that relaxed place. It is just not that easy to speak an unpopular message without prayer.

The fear of speaking causes us to be more concerned with ourselves and how we look than the gospel message and who needs to hear it. It's quite self-centered.

When Moses was given his assignment to go speak to Pharaoh to release God's people, he shrunk back. He worried about his ability to speak. His speech impediment was bigger to him than his assignment. Of course, God didn't see it that way. So God sent

Aaron with him. His people needed their deliverer in spite of his weaknesses.

The writer in the opening scripture is requesting prayer that he would not be afraid to speak and that God would give him the right words to say. He's asking for boldness We can pray this same prayer and God will answer. He has already told us in His word, *But when they hand you over, do not worry about how or what you are to say; for it will be given you in that hour what you are to say. "For it is not you who speak, but it is the Spirit of your Father who speaks in you. Matthew 10:19 NIV*

The idea is to get our attention off of ourselves and on to our God. We are flawed human beings for sure. So we may make mistakes. However it is more important that we deliver the gospel message. It may not be perfect but with God's help, it can be powerful. We must keep first things first.

WRITE IN THE SAND:

Has there been a time when you should've spoke up and your didn't? What happened?

_____

_____

_____

_____

When is the last time you shared the gospel with a stranger? What makes you afraid to speak on behalf of Christ?

GO FEARLESS:

Share the gospel message with a stranger in an elevator, in the grocery store, on social media or in the bank, etc. Prepare ahead of time what you will say. But do it this week.

DAY 10

GET A CLUE

For God hath not given us the spirit of fear; but of power, and of love, and of a sound mind.. II Timothy 1:7 KJV

God has not given us a spirit of fear. So we must have gotten it from somewhere. If God didn't give it to us, who did? It comes from the enemy of our souls to keep us from destiny. Ugly, nasty fear is his weapon of choice. He uses what works. He builds a blockade in our mind as obstacles to God's plan for us.

Fear of speaking keeps you from ministering, teaching, preaching and prophesying. Fear of failure, keeps you from taking a risk to do something really wild and unconventional for God. Fear of rejection keeps you from new relationships and developing intimacy in old ones. And the list goes on. The enemy's mission is to stop you. So he will use a targeted fear to hold you back. He is not random in his selection.

When countries go to war, they study their enemy. They have to know their enemies weaknesses and strengths So turn this question on yourself. If you were the enemy, how would you attack you? It will help you determine what exactly God wants you to do for his kingdom. If you are afraid of speaking, that's a clue that God may use you to speak on his behalf. If you are afraid of rejection, that's an indication that the Lord may want to use you in building relationships. And so on...

Know this, God does not excuse us because we are afraid. He expects that we would do what we are called to do. Fear is not a free pass to escape your assignment. God expects we would do it afraid. Keep going through the shadows because God expects us to. If He expects us to that means He has made it possible. We are fully armed with everything that we need to do whatever He requires.

WRITE IN THE SAND:

What is that God is expecting you to do that causes you apprehension?

_____

_____

_____

_____

_____

_____

_____

GO FEARLESS

Pray against the Spirit of fear in your own life. Discern your purpose and do something toward purpose. If you will one day build a school, then write the plan for it. If you feel called to missions, study the targeted country. Learn something about the people and their culture. Be activated by your purpose.

DAY 11

THE FIGHT IS NOT OVER

"Go, gather together all the Jews who are in Susa, and fast for me. Do not eat or drink for three days, night or day. I and my attendants will fast as you do. When this is done, I will go to the king, even though it is against the law. And if I perish, I perish."
Esther 4:16 NIV

What a statement! "If I die, I die!" This was a bold declaration for the young queen to make. She was willing to do what God was asking her. She was afraid. But she would do it, anyway. Racial persecution was prevalent in the town where she lived. The hearts of the people were consumed with hate – one people against another. The teenage found her relatives were targeted by those in charge. Her uncle was an activist for her people. He heard about this one crooked administrator who had planned to kill all of her family. Because this young girl had married the king, her uncle asked her to get involved. There was something she could do to stop the oppression of her people. At first, she didn't want to get involved because she knew it could cost her life. She was just too afraid.

She tried to explain it to her uncle. But he was agitated by her resistance. She was so torn. Her uncle spoke sternly to her. "Don't think that the racism in the heart of this nation will not affect you because of your position. God will send help to us from another place but you and those close to you will be killed. Have you considered that perhaps the position you hold is for this reason and season?"

Esther gave one of the most impactful responses... "If I die, I die". The statement uncovers her fear. Her fear was attached to the dreaded outcome. She didn't want to approach the king because it was against the law. She could lose her life for such an offense. But Esther surrendered her fear. She let it go for the call on her life. God had put her in this position for this cause. Not for her own delight or comfort.

How do we overcome? We must let go of the outcome. Your response and mine must be "I was put here for this. It was for this hour that I was put into this world. I am here by design. And God will back me up. We must proceed with the assignment, leaving the outcome up to God.

WRITE IN THE SAND:

Write about a time when you thought something wasn't going to work out, but it did.

_____

_____

_____

_____

_____

_____

_____

_____

GO FEARLESS

Look for an opportunity to defend someone today either personally or by writing a letter to a politician, school board, CEO, clergy, businessman, etc.

DAY 12

FEAR IS SIN

But the fearful, and unbelieving, and the abominable, and murderers, and whoremongers, and sorcerers, and idolaters, and all liars, shall have their part in the lake which burneth with fire and brimstone: which is the second death. Revelation 21:8 KJV

The "fearful" lead the list of those who will be burned with fire and brimstone. It seems a bit unfair. Why should those that are timid and afraid be listed with murderers? Because fear is sinful.

If we understand fear, it really does makes sense. When fear appears in your life, there is a choice we make between ourselves and God. To choose fear is to choose ourselves over God. It happens when we measure a situation and decide that God is not enough.

Fear rallies us to stand in opposition against God by diminishing His power. We simply do not trust Him. We exalt self and "perceived" safety over Christ. We become lords of our own lives unwilling to trust the Lord of lords. We flat out refuse his instruction. We won't do what he asks or say what he tells us to say. It's just too risky. So we choose us over God. And stay within our safe spaces.

In Numbers 13. God had promised the children of Israel a land flowing with milk and honey. The 12 spies were sent by Moses to spy out the land. Ten of them returned full of fear. Their response: Yes, the land is plentiful. It's all that God said that it is. However we cannot do what God says we could do - take this land. There are giants in the land. **"They are stronger than we."** They had measured themselves against the circumstance and came up short. We are grasshoppers in our own eyes and in their eyes also. "We are not able to go up against them." What a disastrous report! God had told them they were to go up against them. Their victory was already secured. But fear would not allow them to obey God. And God was angry. He wanted to bless and prosper them but their fear was bigger than their view of Him. It cost them everything.

When we allow fear to rule, it will always cause us to disobey our God. Fear is evil and puts us in opposition against God. Recognize fear for what it is and kill it in your life.

WRITE IN THE SAND:

What has kept you from obeying an instruction from God?

_____

_____

_____

_____

_____

_____

_____

GO FEARLESS

Repent of fear and disobedience. Practice fearlessness by apologizing to someone you've offended. If you don't know who that is, pray and the Lord will reveal.

DAY 13

GOD IN YOUR EQUATION

And in the fourth watch of the night Jesus went unto them, walking on the sea. And when the disciples saw him walking on the sea, they were troubled, saying, It is a spirit; and they cried out for fear. But straightway Jesus spake unto them, saying, Be of good cheer; it is I; be not afraid. And Peter answered him and said, Lord, if it be thou, bid me come unto thee on the water. And he said, Come. And when Peter was come down out of the ship, he walked on the water, to go to Jesus. But when he saw the wind boisterous, he was afraid; and beginning to sink, he cried, saying, Lord, save me. And immediately Jesus stretched forth his hand, and caught him, and said unto him, O thou of little faith, wherefore didst thou doubt? Matthew 14:25-31 KJV

Matthew 14:25-31 When Peter said to Jesus, "if it is you, Lord, bid me to come", he stepped out on God's Word. God was central to his equation - but the moment he **saw** the winds and the waves, he began to sink. I think he saw more than the winds and waves. I think he also saw himself. Jesus was not in the picture that he focused on. So he began to panic.

The winds and waves weren't relevant to his ability to walk on water. He was defying natural laws. He shouldn't have been able to walk even if the sun had been shining and the storm was absent.

The storm was raging before he ever got out of the boat. So the winds and waves were just a distraction to get him to look at himself. And it worked. Peter had essentially left Jesus out of his equation. And turned his attention to himself. "I can't walk on water." He focused on his own capability. He forgot that it was Jesus who bid him to come. And he began to sink.

He was only able to walk because of God's power. The Lord was right there with him.

You don't have to be the strongest, the wisest, nor the one with the most influence, money or power. You only need to be the one who the Lord is with.

In I Samuel 17, we find Goliath terrorizing all of Israel. The entire army of soldiers are trembling with intimidation because of Goliath. He stood over 9 feet, railing and mocking Israel. Even their king was fearful. But a little shepherd boy had God in his equation, "Who is this uncircumcised Philistine who defies the armies of **THE LIVING GOD**?" He was sure that he could win because of his equation. He had seen this equation before with a bear and a lion. God always wins!

I can do all things through Christ which strengthens me. With God all things are possible. Things that are impossible with men are possible with God. Through my God I am able to run through a troop and leap over a wall. We are more than conquerors through Him that loved us. In every one of these "fearless" scriptures, God is the object/source of our power. Magnify God and minimize myself. It is not enough to minimize myself – I must also magnify my God.

We often quote the scripture – resist the devil and he will flee from you. We can't just resist Satan, we must first submit to God. God absolutely must be in our equation.

If you have sized yourself up against whatever you are facing and come up short, ultimately it's because you have eliminated God from your equation. Without Him, you do not stand a chance.

WRITE IN THE SAND:

Do you consult the Lord every time you need to make a decision? Why/Why not?

_____

_____

_____

_____

Think about the present storm you face. Will God show up for you? Why/Why not?

_____

_____

_____

_____

GO FEARLESS

Draw a picture of yourself walking on water in a storm. Don't worry if you aren't artistic. Just draw it as you see it in your mind. Even if it's with stick figures.

DAY 14

GOD IS FOR US

What then shall we say to these things, If God is for us, who can be against us? Romans 8:31 NIV

What do we have to fear? Psalm 27:1 says it like this: The LORD is my light and my salvation-- whom shall I fear? The LORD is the stronghold of my life-- of whom shall I be afraid? If we really believe that God is for us, then fear is irrelevant, obsolete if you will.

During the Civil War, Abraham Lincoln was purportedly asked if God was on his side. His famous response was "Sir, my concern is not whether God is on our side; my greatest concern is to be on God's side, for God is always right.

What a statement! Am I on God's side? That's something to contemplate. Because If I am, then of course, He is on my side. I cannot presume that God is on my side or for me just because I want Him to be. I must reflect honestly and openly to determine if I am in right standing with God or if I have stepped out of His will.

Do I find myself in sin? Sin will always lead us away from God. Am I leaning on my own understanding and choosing my own way? If so, then God is not on my side. Have I even sought the Lord for counsel in this situation? My confession that Jesus is Lord must be made manifest in my life.

I have a promise not only that God is for me, but if we go up a few verses in Romans, v. 28 Paul says, "And we know that in all things God works for the good of those who love him, who have been called according to his purpose. For those God foreknew he also predestined to be conformed to the image of his Son, that he might be the firstborn among many brothers and sisters. And those he predestined, he also called; those he called, he also justified; those he justified, he also glorified.

Do I love Him enough to surrender my life's choices to Him? God does not require perfection. He requires a fully committed relationship. That's what righteousness is. We are justified by faith. So we don't have to be "good" enough. We just have to love him enough to do what He asks.

WRITE IN THE SAND:

On a scale of 1 to 10 with 10 being the most obedient, how obedient to God are you? Explain your answer.

_____

_____

_____

Am I on God's side in this situation? Why/Why not? If not what do I need to change to make sure I am on His side?

_____

_____

_____

GO FEARLESS

Memorize Romans 8:31

DAY 15

PEOPLE PLEASING

Fear of man will prove to be a snare, but whoever trusts in the LORD is kept safe. Proverbs 29:25 NIV

In God, whose word I praise— in God I trust and am not afraid. What can mere mortals do to me? Psalm 56:4 NIV

Why do we fear people to the point of having to please them at our own expense? Do we think that they can harm us? Perhaps we worry that they have more power than we do; or maybe we fear they will reject us. No matter what the reason is -at its root is fear.

There is a natural tension between fear and faith. We don't like to feel the discomfort of it. People pleasing is a prison. Sometimes we miss out on what God wants to do in in our lives because we go to people, expecting them to give us what we need emotionally, instead of God. Certainly, God will work through the people He puts in our lives to help us, but we need to look to Him for approval, acceptance and wisdom.

There are essentially 3 ills here: First and foremost, we are called to be God pleasers, not men pleasers. Our God is sovereign. As the Creator of the entire universe, He trumps all others. He is Alpha and Omega, the beginning and the end. He is omniscient, omnipotent, and omnipresent. We do not possess the ability to see past this moment but God can see through to the end of time. Not only does He have more power and ability than any human but He is more kind and loving. We can trust Him over any man.

Secondly, if we depend on the opinions of others, how will

we emerge into the wonderful creatures we were designed to be? If we do everything for the benefit of others, how can we know our true selves? We all have unique ideas and desires that should not be stuffed to appease someone else.

It is simply wrong to change yourself to accommodate others. Don't allow yourself to be defined by others. You are who God says you are, not who people want you to be.

Finally, What value is it in being like everyone else or even just 1 someone else? Be comfortable with being yourself. You have a lot to offer. You are God's peculiar treasure. His chosen vessel. It's expected that you would be different. Learn to accept yourself and celebrate your uniqueness. We were created differently on purpose. Let's just live the amazing lives that we were born to live.

WRITE IN THE SAND:

Do you find yourself telling people what they want to hear? If yes, is it all people or just certain people? Why? Who?

_____

_____

_____

_____

Can you tell people the truth, even if it means they will be mad at you?   Yes   No   Sometimes

Tap into your true self. Write a list of all the. things you like. Include favorite color, foods, hobbies, music, books, etc

_____

_____

_____

_____

_____

GO FEARLESS

Commit to being who God wants you to be. Don't stuff or hide who you really are. Practice saying no when you mean no. Tell people the truth in love. Be authentic.

DAY 16

FEAR OF LACK

Do not be anxious about anything, but in everything, by prayer and petition, with thanksgiving, present your requests to God.
Philippians 4:6 NIV

The bill collectors call relentlessly. And it seems there is not enough to satisfy their requests. What usually happens, is we often give into our dreads. Filled with anxiety, we make even more poor decisions. We do a number of things out of fear. We get into more debt by borrowing from one creditor to pay the other. We avoid their calls all together. We make false promises to appease their demands.

Matthew 10:31 says So don't be afraid; you are worth more than many sparrows. God takes care of the little sparrow; every morning fresh worms are available for the birds. Certainly God can take care of you. Release the anxiety. Trust Him. Let go of whatever worries and concerns you may have. David said, I have never seen the righteous forsaken or His seed begging bread. If what David is saying is true, then we only need to remain the righteous. God knows our every need. And He will see that every need is met. He is my Shepherd and I shall not lack.

God is Jehovah Jireh, which means "the Lord our provider" There is nothing too hard for God. Nothing out of His reach. St. Matthew reminds us "Seek God first". All the other things will be added to us. But only as we seek Him as our source. Our hearts should align to His. That means we only what He wants for us, trusting that He has a plan.

We rely on Him to lead us where we ought to be. If we are his, our steps are ordered. He will guide us into the provision that

He has set for us. Trust Him.

Whether you mismanaged your way into a mess or you just don't make enough to make the ends meet, the truth is that you can't lose God. He is with you even in financial straits. Pray, seek His wisdom, and obey His instruction. That is the only way out. It may take a while, but if you stay consistent, you will see your way through. God does care about every financial decision you need to make. Let Him lead you out of trouble.

WRITE IN THE SAND:

What is your biggest financial struggle? Have you been a good steward over the resources God has given you?

_____

_____

_____

_____

What do you need to change in the way you handle money?

_____

_____

_____

_____

GO FEARLESS

Start a savings account for emergencies. Sell things that you don't need to put aside $1,000 in this account. Then use it **only** for emergencies. Always pray before using it. Work on being a better steward of the resources God has given you.

DAY 17

DOCTOR'S REPORT

Thou shalt not be afraid for the terror by night; nor for the arrow that flieth by day; Nor for the pestilence that walketh in darkness; nor for the destruction that wasteth at noonday. A thousand shall fall at thy side, and ten thousand at thy right hand; but it shall not come nigh thee.

Psalms 91:5-7 KJV

I sat anxiously awaiting the doctor to come out with my results. I had an abnormal mammogram. There were lumps in both breasts. I had to come back for more tests. This time I had to take an ultrasound and another mammogram. The tech went to get the doctor while I sat in the cool waiting area with half of a paper robe.

My mind wandered, "What if it was the c word?" I started imagining what I would do. Who I would tell. I started preparing in my mind as if I was expecting it. "I won't cry", I told myself. Interrupting my toxic thoughts, the doctor called me back. The lumps were benign. I breathed a deep sigh of relief. I wanted to collapse into the tears that I said I wouldn't release. I had been so tense. But why? It hit me. I was afraid. Sometimes we don't like to admit when we find ourselves in fear. There I was curled up in a ball of anxiety. Not literally, but figuratively. And I did actually catch myself not trusting God.

I was afraid of the pestilence. I was afraid that it would prevail over me. God is a healer. I know that. But fear snuck in while I wasn't paying attention. Whether the report was positive or not, I should always expect a good report. I should always believe for the best. And even when the negative report comes, I should believe that God is victor over it.

I don't have to be afraid of sickness or disease. Jesus already handled that on the cross. Fear doesn't dismiss sickness; it won't go away. But faith can certainly access my healing.

The same is true for you. Always expect a good report and in those rare times when it doesn't come, expect healing. Hope in Jesus. Believe in His power.

When bad news comes people often ask, "Where is God?" Be assured. God is with you in the midst of good news and bad. He doesn't run away because you are diagnosed with something. He promises to be with us until the ends of the earth. So no matter what we go through, let us go in faith. And let's not hold on so tightly to this life. Our life on this earth is temporary. None of us will remain here forever. So what is there to fear? We go from here to eternity, where there is no pain or sickness. No tears. So whether we are healed on this side or on the other side, we still win.

WRITE IN THE SAND:

With what infirmities are you currently challenged? Do you someone(s) who is worse off than you?

List their names.

_____

_____

_____

_____

Write healing scriptures on index cards. Post them in your bathroom.

_____

_____

_____

_____

GO FEARLESS

Choose someone on your sick list. Visit them and pray for them. If you don't know anyone personally, visit a nursing home or hospital.

DAY 18

STORMY WEATHER

He stilled the storm to a whisper; the waves of the sea were hushed. Psalm 107:29

As a little girl, I remember the booming roar of the thunder and the lightning flashing and crackling the sky. The noisy pair frightened me. My grandmother would make us all come in and sit still on the floor in the dark. She would cut off the television and all appliances. She said that God was busy doing His work. It made me wonder, "How often did God work? What kind of work was He doing? And why was it so loud?"

What I've come to realize as an adult is that every storm that comes is not from God. In St. Mark 4:37-39, the disciples were caught and tossed around by a terrible storm as Jesus slept. They awakened Him and Jesus rebuked the storm. So we know those violent winds and waves were not the work of God.

On the contrary, In the book of Jonah, verse 4, we read, *Then the LORD sent a great wind on the sea, and such a violent storm arose that the ship threatened to break up.* **Now, this was God doing His work. He was in pursuit of Jonah.**

Storms are different. No two are the same. And they last for varying lengths of time. **Jesus said, "In the world you shall have tribulation."** Know that many storms come through no fault of our own. When storms come we won't always know if they are from God or not. But we can always know that He is mighty in power. When you are hidden in Him, you are able to handle even the fiercest storm that arises in your life. Sometimes it's a false accusation, or an offense from a close friend or family member. Perhaps the storm is a financial crisis that you can't seem to get out of it. Maybe you are in the midst of a lawsuit. ***Whatever your***

storm is, God is still your God. He loves you so much. His love is not diminished for you whether He sent the storm or not. Jesus sits at the right hand of the Father making intercession for you. Did you get that? Jesus is praying about the trouble or trial that you are in right now. He's praying you through to victory. What better person to have praying for you?!

Every person on the earth will enter a storm of some kind at some point in their life. When it comes to you, remember that you are loved even when you don't feel it. Know that the storm is temporary. This too shall pass. And trust God's love and presence in the midst of it. He is with you in every season of your life. You don't have to sit still in the dark. God can do His work in you. Receive the light of His love. Everything will work out for your good.

WRITE IN THE SAND:

Look over your life. List one storm that God sent and one that He did not send. How did you feel?

_____

_____

_____

What waves do you need hushed in your life presently? Can you discern if your present storm is from God or not?

_____

_____

_____

_____

_____

_____

_____

GO FEARLESS

Find someone going through something similar to you. Sow a seed, buy a gift, or provide a service for them. Minister God's love to that person.

DAY 19

CRITICAL CONDITION

Examine yourselves to see whether you are in the faith; test yourselves. Do you not realize that Christ Jesus is in you--unless, of course, you fail the test? II Corinthians 13:5

There is a lot of talk about our so called "haters". The term is so broadly used that its definition sweeps almost everyone into the category. However every person is not your hater. In fact, most people are not hating on you. Just because people don't agree with you or see something in the same way that you do, that doesn't constitute them as a hater. They may see something in your life that needs to change. We all are subject to criticism, whether constructive or not.

The real question is how do we deal with those who are critical of us? Not all criticism is true. So we don't just receive everything that is said about us. But neither is all criticism false. And so we don't just throw it all out. Examine it. Pray about it and ask the Lord what is it that we are to get out of it.

It takes courage to receive constructive criticism. Most people don't handle it very well. They think that correction equals rejection. They become offended and fall back into old patterns of fear. We weren't born in perfection. We were born into sin. Therefore we are subject to error. Being willing to face up to that is huge. Maturity is growing to the place where we can take responsibility for our actions, the good, the bad, and the ugly.

It's sad when a person is criticized and instead of examining themselves, they want to find something wrong with the person delivering the message. This is done to disqualify what was said. But that's kind of silly, because God **always** speaks through flawed beings. So there is always something wrong with the speaker.

Ignoring a criticism, because we are upset with the person giving it, is not mature or wise. We shouldn't think in terms of all good or all bad. No one person is either. We should be open to receive truth from whomever God wants to use. It really is for our benefit. It's the way we grow.

WRITE IN THE SAND:

Have you rejected a criticism from someone? What was it? Was there some truth to it?

_____

_____

_____

_____

Could any part of it have been from God? Which part?

_____

_____

_____

_____

GO FEARLESS

Be brave enough to ask a few close friends, what can you do to be a better person? Pray about it. Receive it if there is the slightest chance that it could be true and work on yourself in that area. Chances are even if you can't see it, you will once you start to make the adjustments.

DAY 20

BROKEN LOVE

*If an enemy were insulting me, I could endure it;
if a foe were rising against me, I could hide. But it is you, a man
like myself, my companion, my close friend, with whom I once
enjoyed sweet fellowship at the house of God, as we walked
about among the worshipers. Psalm 55:12-14 NIV*

It is a difficult thing to walk through a betrayal, whether it is a lover, relative or close friend. When it happens, fear invades your heart. Fear of losing the relationship, fear that there is something wrong with us, and the fear of loving someone new, all demand entrance.

As human beings, we generally don't love like we should and we break covenant like empty bottles. And boy does it hurt the person on the receiving end! Especially when the offended person is left to wonder what was it that they did to deserve such treatment?

The psalmist shares with us his pain. He seems to be shocked by the behavior of his ex-friend. "We worshipped together", he said. I did not expect this from you. An enemy? yes! But not you." Broken hearted he cries out to God to avenge him. "Death to my enemy!" He prays.

Jesus had endured betrayal by Judas. The thieving treasurer sold Jesus out for a few coins. But Jesus dealt with Judas based on His love for Judas. It was not based in retaliation to Judas's tainted love. When Judas brought the accusers, Jesus called him friend and allowed himself to be kissed by the one offering him the cup of suffering. He knew full well what Judas would do. Yet, Jesus was still teaching and it was for our learning. We are never to render evil for evil. Good is what we offer in exchange for the evil we receive. We are encouraged to forgive, love, and bless those that harm us .

When our hearts are left torn in pieces by some relationship that we valued, we are to run to the Lord for healing. He knows how to put us back together again.

Forgive. And love. That may mean reconciliation, in most cases it does. So keep a clean heart. Hold on to love. Love never fails. Let God do what He needs to do in your heart. The sacrifices of God are a broken heart and a broken and contrite spirit.

WRITE IN THE SAND:

How do you apply Psalm 51:17 to your life? Do you have any leftover hurt? Who hurt you?

_____

_____

_____

_____

_____

Do you react like David or like Jesus when hurt by someone you love? What has been your response in the past?

_____

_____

_____

_____

GO FEARLESS

Pray for the person that harmed you every day this week. At the end of the week, write a love note to that person but don't mail it unless you feel led to do so.

DAY 21

SLEEP IN HEAVENLY PEACE

When you lie down, you will not be afraid; When you lie down, your sleep will be sweet. Proverbs 3:24 NIV

Insomnia can wreck a person's life. And many times it is a result of fear. Counting sheep never worked for me. Sometimes I would lie awake, trying my best to go to sleep; but my mind just wouldn't cooperate. It regurgitated the day's worries. "How is this going to work out? What will I do about that? If this happen, then what will I do?" And even though I had no answers for it, it seemed to stay on repeat.

It's funny that the mind never has to be trained to worry. It is automatic like a default setting. In fact, the training is on the opposite end of the spectrum. We have to learn how NOT to worry.

Whether we realize it or not, worry is fear. It's fear that things won't work out. Some say it's faith that things won't work out. It's the belief that everything will come crashing down on our heads.

Worry never helped anyone. It causes illness and robs us of our peace. The scriptures give us a remedy for worry. It is prayer. Paul says in Philippians 4:6-7 (KJV) Be careful for nothing; but in everything by prayer and supplication with thanksgiving let your requests be made known unto God. And the peace of God, which passeth all understanding, shall keep your hearts and minds through Christ Jesus.

Be full of care, concern, or worry about nothing! In the Message version, it says, "Don't fret or worry! Instead of worrying, pray!"

Praying about our troubles is the best way to handle them.

Hand them over to God. He actually possesses the power to do something about them. He will give us peace that transcends understanding. As we rest in Him, He will keep guard over our hearts. This is the promise we have in this proverb. Peace and rest come as a result of wisdom.

If He is really Lord over our lives, then we need to let Him govern them. We are no good at being in charge. There's a bonus, He doesn't sleep or slumber. So no need of us both staying awake.

WRITE IN THE SAND:

What are you worried about?

_____

_____

_____

_____

_____

_____

_____

GO FEARLESS

When you go to sleep tonight, listen to a peaceful worship song. Let it resonate in your spirit. Release each care to the Lord one by one.

DAY 22

BE STILL

Be still, and know that I am God: I will be exalted among the heathen, I will be exalted in the earth. Psalms 46:10 KJV

We are always rushing and in a hurry – just busy, being busy. We stand at the microwave demanding its haste. We are annoyed with the speed of our computers. No matter how fast we get them to go, we want them to move faster. We even blow our horns haphazardly at the person in the fast lane, insisting that they speed up. We rush through life at a whizzing pace. Then God whispers from Heaven, "Be still..." Wait, what? As if we don't understand what it means to be still. Maybe we have forgotten.

Stillness is a discipline. Stillness means to be patient and pause. It is to give preference to God, as to stop in reverence as He is slowly ushered to take His highest seat. Be still means to stand back in trust. It is only in stillness that we can truly know God. The knowledge of God is released like the juice from ripened fruit.

We watch Him do what He does without our assistance or interference. He's God enough to handle our lives. If we are consumed with our own busyness and with our agenda, we will miss what God wants to do. We will forfeit His opportunity to be glorified and our opportunity to know His power in that situation.

Many times God requires our cooperation with Him but in those exceptional times when God says, BE still, we have to stand back and watch His miracle working power in action. Rest in His sovereignty.

It takes courage to be still. Usually God says be still at a time when we want to do something. We've become so accustomed to our busyness that we feel like we have to do something. When a mom in labor has dilated to ten centimeters, there is this urge to push – but the doctor says not yet. At that point, mom is told to wait or be still. And then at the height of her contraction, she is released to push.

In full confidence and without fear, we are admonished to wait on God. We are not to rush ahead, no matter how anxious we get. He doesn't need us to do anything. The eternal God knows the exact time to step in.

We may wonder if He has forgotten – He hasn't. We may even talk ourselves into believing that God didn't really say that – He did. We have to remember that He is the King of the World and we are just created beings. He knows what He is doing. So we can relax and be still, knowing He's got this. We aren't to push until we are released.

WRITE IN THE SAND:

Are you always in a hurry? Are your prayers rushed and sporadic?

_____

_____

_____

Is there a deadline approaching that God seems to be ignoring? What is it? How will you handle it?

_____
_____
_____
_____
_____
_____
_____

GO FEARLESS

Today, go and sit by a lake, river, or other body of water. Sit and listen for God to speak. Don't say anything. Just wait on Him to speak to you. Record what you hear Him saying.

DAY 23

HE IS WITH ME

Have not I commanded you? Be strong and courageous. Do not be afraid; do not be discouraged, for the Lord your God will be with you wherever you go. Joshua 1:9 NIV

Moses was dead. Joshua was the new leader. He had been given a direction and a promise that God would be with him. How he was to do it hadn't been discussed. He was to simply lead without fear. "Don't be sad or fearful", the passage from the very first verse seems to repeat itself.

The new commander of the Israeli army had to submit himself under God's command. And the promise was sure. God would be with Him wherever he went. Can you imagine that? God tells you, I am going to be with you wherever you go. Wouldn't the promise alone make you brave enough to do whatever God asked?

Joshua was to take the people across the Jordan River. The river was overflowing its banks. God said cross it and be brave about doing it. No method was offered just yet. The promise that God will be with him wherever he goes was enough. The Lord would not withdraw his presence.

In Genesis, Joseph's story is an amazing one. The short version is that he was envied by his brothers, thrown into a pit, sold into slavery, and falsely imprisoned. Then he is elevated to government leader, There appears a refrain, "And the Lord was with Joseph." It is the reason for his success. That is to be the refrain of our lives as well. It's the testimony of victory. When the Lord is with us, we are loaded. We are strengthened. We have every resource at our hand. There is no shortage of supply. Nothing is lacking because God is more than enough

You may find yourself standing at the banks with a word to go over. Maybe you don't know the methodology or strategy. God will answer. Be at peace. Don't fret. God's promise to be with us is enough.

WRITE IN THE SAND:

What does it mean to you to be courageous? What are you facing today?

_____

_____

_____

_____

How can you face it without fear?

_____

_____

_____

_____

GO FEARLESS

Write a song. The song should tell how God is with you wherever you go.

_____
_____
_____
_____
_____
_____
_____
_____
_____
_____
_____
_____
_____
_____
_____

DAY 24

GOOD GRIEF

Brothers and sisters, we do not want you to be uninformed about those who sleep in death, so that you do not grieve like the rest of mankind, who have no hope.   I Thessalonians 4:13 NIV

Funerals are excruciating. No one "wants" to be there. We find ourselves compelled by our love for the deceased. When a loved one dies, there is a lot to process. Emotions are all over the place: regret, fear, anger, hurt and sadness. Often we are not sure what to feel. The air is thick with uncertainty.

As a rule, people are afraid of death. Funerals force us to look at our own mortality. We are, many times, too fearful to face it otherwise.   We are spiritual beings living on earth for a predetermined time. It's common sense that if a person enters the earth realm he/she must also exit. However, that knowledge doesn't make it any easier to handle.

Jesus attended funerals. In one instance, we find him arriving late for his friend, Lazarus's funeral. The scripture says, He wept (John 11:35). But why? Was he grieving for his friend? But if He was on the way to raise Lazarus from the dead, why would he cry? Did he weep because those around him didn't believe? Was He emotional about his own death which was imminent? Was his heart grieved because of sin that brought death into the world?

I think it was all of those things. Jesus did indeed express deep compassion for those suffering. He was sympathetic to the two sisters. He felt their pain. He wept because he entered their sorrow. He wept because those around Him did not believe. His tears were compounded by sin. His act of raising Lazarus would be the catalyst to his own death. Jesus wept.

On the other hand, He knew the promise that lie ahead of him. He knew that He would call Lazarus forth. There would be laughter, and joy. He also knew that He also would be resurrected from the dead. Because He is death's kryptonite. Life is in Him. He would save His people from their sins. There was something good in those tears. Perhaps tears of hope for He is the Hope of Glory. Tears of promise. He is the promise keeper. Tears of victory that death would no longer triumph over God's people.

He wants us to know that death for the believer is never final. There is hope on the other side. Jesus encourages us, Let not your heart be troubled. You believe in God. Believe also in me. I go to prepare a place for you. In my Father's house are many mansions.

These were the comforting words He left us as He made his exit from the earth. We would do well to remember that death is temporary. It is our passage way into the eternal life.

This life isn't all there is. There is so much more in store. Yes it's difficult when we lose a loved one. But that's not the end of the story. Those who know God will live again.

WRITE IN THE SAND:

Have you had a loss in the past year? How have you handled it?

_____

_____

_____

_____

Use a separate piece of paper. Write a letter to God to express your grief. Tell him all that you are feeling. And let Him speak back to you.

GO FEARLESS

Reach out to someone who is grieving. Send them a card, flowers, or gift. Show love and concern for them.

DAY 25

OUT OF CONTROL

Trust in the LORD with all your heart and lean not on your own understanding; in all your ways submit to him, and he will make your paths straight. Proverbs 3:5-6 NIV

"Let go and let God!" This is one of the most over-quoted clichés in Christianity. But its essence is crucial to growing in intimacy with the Lord. Yet how does one let go?

Some people have to be in control. They have to know what's next. They often have a plan for their life that is all mapped out. Losing control can be frightening for them. However as believers we are not asked to lose control, but to surrender it. We are asked to lay it down as a perpetual act of worship. We don't just leave control abstractly into the hands of anyone who picks it up. But we lay it intentionally in the hands of our trustworthy God.

Letting go is about releasing control of your life and the way that you think things should turn out. It means trusting God's leadership. That can be pretty intimidating. God's direction doesn't always make sense. It's risky and can leave you feeling uncertain.

When we are in control we hold on to the way we want the ending to turn out. We pray for that particular outcome. We want to force God to do it our way. And we even feel like God aborts us if we don't get the outcome we prayed for. Fearlessness is about trusting God with the outcome. It means jumping in with both feet with your eyes wide open. It may not turn out like you want it, but it will turn out like you need.

Think about this, the 3 Hebrew boys told the king that they

would not bow and their God was able to deliver them; but even if He didn't, they still would not bow. They let go. In the midst of his tremendous loss, Job said, "Though he slay me, yet will I trust Him." That's how you let go. Even Jesus prayed to the Father, Let this cup pass from me...Nevertheless not my will, but thy will be done. That's letting go. We must abandon control to a loving and faithful God. He knows what's best. He is the one who can see past the moment.

It's time for the people of God to be brave enough to be out of control. So let go.

WRITE IN THE SAND:

What part of your life is God asking you to release, right now? Why do you find it difficult?

_____

_____

_____

_____

Jesus, Job, and the 3 Hebrew boys, all responded to something that was difficult and physically challenging. Study their stories. Compare it to yours.

_____

_____

_____

GO FEARLESS

Go on a prayer walk. Let the Lord minister to you about His Lordship of your life. Give Him something value to you to symbolically let go of your life.

DAY 26

CHAMELEON

But now, this is what the LORD says-- he who created you, Jacob, he who formed you, Israel: "Do not fear, for I have redeemed you; I have summoned you by name; you are mine. Isaiah 43:1 NIV

Fear is a chameleon. It changes shape, color, and expression. It is not always about shaking in your boots. It's not the teeth-shattering, nail-biting type of emotion that we see in the movies. Fear is manifested in different ways. Sometimes we don't even recognize fear when it comes. There are times when fear is calm, but sad. It can come in so subtly that you don't even know it's there.

The general definition of fear is: an unpleasant emotion caused by the belief that someone or something is dangerous, likely to cause pain or suffering. Of course we know anxiety and worry as fear that something bad is going to happen to us. We can feel it in the pit of our bellies. It makes us uneasy. But it doesn't stop there. Fear is sneaky and transforms itself to penetrate our hearts. In order to activate the word in our lives, we must be awake to fear. It is imperative that we recognize it in all of our forms.

<u>Jealousy/envy</u> is fear that someone else will have more or achieve more than you. Or that you will be left behind.

<u>Doubt</u> is fear that situations will not work out or turn out well. It is faith in failure. It is fear that God won't show up.

<u>Discouragement</u> is fear that there is no hope. It is a result of an expectation that did not pan out. It comes as a result of holding on to the outcome.

<u>Depression</u> is fear that life will never get better. It is the belief that you are doomed to your present life situation. There is no way out.

<u>Stress</u> is fear that what you have is less than what is needed. The demands exceed your resources, whether the resources needed are energy, time, wisdom, finances, or otherwise. You believe that you don't have what you need.

<u>People-pleasing</u> is fear of rejection or not being accepted or liked. In this type of fear, people will lie or be dishonest. People will say what is expected or accepted and not what is true.

Fearlessness is our right. We belong to the most powerful King of the world. He created and formed us without fear. So we were born to be fearless. We somehow picked it up along the way. Even in that, we are redeemed from fear. As His seed, we must stand up to fear no matter what form it takes. Fear shows up to try to consume us. But we won't be caught off guard! We will recognize it when it shows up. We will be Fearless!

WRITE IN THE SAND:

What type of fear are you dealing with this week? Is there more than 1?

_____

_____

_____

_____

_____

_____

_____

_____

GO FEARLESS

What does fear look like? What color is your fear? Draw a picture of the fear that is challenging you. Wear pink this week or something that represents fearlessness to you.

DAY 27

SHAME, SHAME, SHAME

Do not be afraid; you will not be put to shame. Do not fear disgrace; you will not be humiliated. You will forget the shame of your youth and remember no more the reproach of your widowhood. Isaiah 54:4

Shame is fear that you are less than who God created you to be. Fear that you are unlovable, unlikeable or unworthy. Shame makes its home in secrecy. Something "bad" happens and we bury it. It's allowed to fester and grow there. Without secrecy, it's hard for shame to survive. However we try to keep it covered and go about our lives. But it never works out, because it's just not that easy. The enemy absolutely will dig it up and use it against us.

Shame is about who we are. It speaks to our identity. It is the fear that we are not enough. Shame causes us to operate in two personas, my true identity and the false one. The false one is nearly perfect. That's the one we want to share on our social media page. That's the one we want the world to see. "Look at me and applaud me for being a good person, wife, mother, daughter etc. I want the world to see how wonderful I am."

The scripture reminds us, none is good but God. Romans 3:23 says that we all have sinned and fell short of God's glory. We are dysfunctional before we meet Christ. So how does shame maintain its grip on our lives? Shame can only access us through pride. Think about it. We only feel shame because we don't want to be identified with our true selves. We want people to see us blemish-free.

In the late 80's, adultery hit our marriage. My husband and I went through a tough time. And even though he was the one who stepped outside of the relationship, I felt ashamed. Questions loomed over us. What would people think about us? What would they think about me? I felt damaged - that I was the type of person that a man would cheat on. (What type was that? My reasoning was skewed) I felt less than others around me. I wondered what people would think - not only that adultery had touched our lives, but that I stayed in the relationship. Wouldn't they think I was foolish? Those questions were sent to distort my image.

Thank God for Jesus. We went through the process and the Lord healed us completely. We shared our story every chance we got. We put it in a book. Talked about it on television and on radio. We shared it over multiple pulpits. Because the only way to overcome is to own it. Share it, don't hide it. Secrecy keeps us in shame. Openness releases us from it. The scripture says open confession is good for the soul. God has a remedy for shame. We overcome by the blood of the Lamb and the words of our testimony.

The truth of the matter is we are not worthy or good enough outside of Christ. It is in Him that we find our value. So as we own our brokenness and tell our stories we no longer have to feel ashamed.

WRITE IN THE SAND:

Is there something of which you are still ashamed? Be brave enough to write it down.

_____

_____

_____

_____

_____

_____

_____

_____

GO FEARLESS

Choose someone safe (a spouse, mentor, pastor). Share your story with them. Work on growing to the point where you can share your testimony with a stranger.

DAY 28

GOD-FIDENCE

So God created mankind in his own image, in the image of God he created them; male and female he created them. Genesis 1:27

Self-image, self-esteem and self-confidence are the way we see ourselves. It's the way we value ourselves emotionally. The best coaches and motivational speakers tell us that our image of ourselves should be very high. Judge yourselves worthy and deserving. Lift yourself up. "Be confident in yourself!" Love yourself! Then you can accomplish anything.

The trouble with all of this positive thinking is that it doesn't last. Self is at the center. And because we really don't believe our own hype. Our suspicions overtake what we profess out of our mouths. We know the secrets about ourselves. We are the ones who wrestle with the internal truths that underline our lives. We can be positive about it all we want, but we know us.

As women, we especially struggle with our image, always believing that we are too fat, too tall, too short, too something or another. If we are not too much, we believe that we are not enough. Not pretty enough, not thin enough, not smart enough. The voices in our heads are pretty convincing.

So what makes us so spectacular or outstanding or so wonderful? It's really the One that created us. God is miraculous, faithful, kind, trustworthy, powerful, loving, and gracious. And that's not even all there is to Him.

In myself, I am nothing. It's in Christ that I find true value. When I abide in Him, He abides in me. And I can do all things through Christ, not through me. So instead of self-confidence, I need to boost my God-fidence. I am sure of His might. There are no flaws in Him. He is simply amazing.

It doesn't matter if I've put on a couple extra pounds or if I am shorter than I desire to be, or I don't have enough money. The truth is I am fearfully and wonderfully made, created in the image of God. I belong to Him. I find beauty in me because of Him

He created me to be like Him. It's not what I look like on the outside that matters most, it's what I am on the inside.   I am creative, caring, wise, faithful, thoughtful and generous. These are attributes of God. I am my daddy's daughter. Certainly I am not all that I will be, but when He does appear, I will be just like Him. I belong to God and that's what makes me valuable.

WRITE IN THE SAND:

What do you love about yourself? What do you dislike?

_____

_____

_____

_____

_____

_____

_____

What was God thinking when He created you? What attributes did He give you? What talents and strengths to help you complete your assignment?

_____
_____
_____
_____
_____
_____
_____
_____
_____
_____

GO FEARLESS

Repeat this affirmation everyday: I am God's daughter. He has chosen me and I have chosen Him. I am all that He says that I am. I can do all that He says I can do. I will go in every place that He sends me. I walk in full faith. Nothing shall intimidate me. I cancel every demonic assignment and every generational curse over my life. I decree victory in every area of my life. I cast down fear in all its forms. I will not back down, back up or shrink myself. I am a force to be reckoned with – made in the image of God. I am able to run through a troop and leap over a wall. I am a winner and not a loser. I am the head and not the tail. Above only and not beneath. I am able to walk on serpents and scorpions over all the power of Satan. I agree with God's Word therefore I make this declaration in the name of Jesus. I am fearless!

DAY 29

DISTRACTIONS

I am saying this for your benefit, not to place restrictions on you. I want you to do whatever will help you serve the Lord best, with as few distractions as possible. I Corinthians 7:35 NLT

Distractions keep us from our pursuit of God. But what exactly are distractions? Persecutions, trouble, trials to cause you to lose focus. But distractions are not always negative in nature. Sometimes distractions are gifts, promotions, social media, favor, etc. Distractions are all the things that take our attention off God.

We are not ignorant of the enemy's devices. We are fully aware of who he is and what he's up to. So why do we permit his interference in our lives, when the Word says, the gates of hell shall not prevail against us.

The enemy wants to cause your confidence to be shaken and turn you around from the way you are going. The enemy uses little things. It's the little foxes that destroy the vines. Those incidents that aren't so obvious to draw us away from the things of God. It's like the stranger offering a child a treat to draw him away from his mother. The child knows better than to accept a treat from a stranger. But for some reason, he ignores the warning in his spirit and goes for the treat. When he does, he is captured.

We must keep our attention on God regardless of the noise that surrounds us. There is a mission to accomplish, an assignment to complete. We must fix our eyes on Jesus.

Know that distractions will keep us captive to fear and away from purpose. You are called to courage. Keep on your journey to a fearless life. Let nothing obstruct your view.

Every time there is a distraction, there is a fork in the road. We must decide to allow the distraction to sidetrack us or move straight ahead. But it is your decision. Make the decision today and every day to keep moving toward purpose.

WRITE IN THE SAND:

Have you identified any distractions in your life? If so, what are they? How will you deal with them?

_____
_____
_____
_____
_____
_____
_____
_____
_____
_____

GO FEARLESS

Shut down social media, television, web surfing, and all other extra-curricular activity, for a full day, once a week. Use that time to spend in God's presence.

DAY 30

BATTLE SCARS

From henceforth let no man trouble me: for I bear in my body the marks of the Lord Jesus.. Galatians 6:17 KJV

My chin was burst wide open as I hit the concrete. Blood spilled out everywhere. I was rushed to emergency. This injury was a result of fear. I was around 6 years old. I was riding my two-wheeled bike with no training wheels. I was confident, as long as I was riding alone. I would become afraid if someone was riding beside me. My brother knew this. So as siblings do, he decided to ride next to me to taunt me. All of the confidence and ability I had before went out of the window. I began to shake and I lost control of the handle bars and down I went. I received 12 stitches. And 47 years later, I still have that scar.

Scars are reminders, visible testimonies. For every scar – there is a story imprinted in our memory. Paul said, In 2 Corinthians 11:22-27, there were grievous, countless, hardships which marked his career. "In stripes above measure,... in deaths oft. Of the Jews, five times received I forty stripes save one; thrice was I beaten with rods, once was I stoned, thrice I suffered shipwreck, a night and a day have I been in the deep." Remember the stoning at Lystra where he was dragged outside of the city and left for dead. Did he have some scars? What about that snake bite? Did it leave a scar?

Paul said for I bear on my body the marks of Jesus. For His sake and cause, I have received these marks. It was a participation in His suffering.

The least I can do is to live this life to the max. Paul was fearless. He faced some precarious situations and kept getting in the face of them. He didn't stand back. He didn't hide out. He kept getting in the face of fear. Because fear alone is powerless. In and of itself - it can't stop you. Fear is there to intimidate you. Hoping that you won't live the maximized life. Dreading that you will not access this life to the full. "Hold back!", fear screams. " Don't get back up." If you get a scar do not get back in harm's way.

I got back on that bike. As the years, went on, I broke my arm playing kick ball at school. I broke my leg. I've sprained my ankle. Survived car crashes. Come through surgeries. Some of those events produced physical scars, some emotional.

You will get some scars if you serve God. It is inevitable. You can't live life without getting hurt. And if you are going to attend to this fearless life you will be challenged with opportunities to overcome fear. The challenge is will you get back out there? Will you live the maximized life? Don't let hurt cause you to live in a bubble.

Scars say that you are an overcomer. Scars are marks of success. Whatever you had to face, the scar is a reminder that God brought you through it. You made it! It is a mark of a former pain and a symbol that you were healed.

Jesus has scars. Nail prints in his hand. When He looks at His scars, he remembers us. He fearlessly marched toward the cross to gain the love of his life – each of us. He was, is, and always be the most fearless person in the world. His scars are proof of that.

WRITE IN THE SAND:

Do you have any physical or emotional scars? What happened? How have you handled them?

_____

_____

_____

_____

_____

_____

_____

Do you see victory in your scars? How so?

_____

_____

_____

GO FEARLESS

Tell someone the story of your scar. And how God brought you through. Magnify the Lord as you share your story.

DAY 31

GIVE BIRTH

Therefore go and make disciples of all nations, baptizing them in the name of the Father and of the Son and of the Holy Spirit, Matthew 28:19 NIV

Satan is our archenemy. And his weapon of choice is fear. It we cower in fear, others will, too. But if we stand up in faith, it too is contagious. We can affect how others deal with the fear in their lives. We have to decide how our lives will influence others – for evil or for good.

We are called to live in community with others. We must share our substance, but much more than that – we are asked to share our lives. The elder women are called to pour into the lives of the younger (Titus 2:4).

As I grow in courage and boldness, I call my spiritual daughters to do the same. I won't let myself use fear as an excuse, neither will I allow them to do so . My battle cry to them is, "Follow me as I follow and trust in Christ." We trudge ahead in obedience. They may "feel" fear, but they won't let it stop them. Feelings are fickle and not to be relied upon.

The only way to kill fear is to rally the troops against it. It's the 'each one, reach one' philosophy. You tell someone, they tell someone else, who tells someone else, and so on. It's the way we make disciples. Our modern day term is mentoring.

You have been immunized against fear by the Word of God. It is now your responsibility to bring others alongside. Teach your sons and daughters. Give them passages to read and study. Ask them to take notes about what they've read. **Discuss it. Pray with them. Memorize scripture. Challenge them to application.** Ask them to journal. Cry with them. Laugh with them. Fellowship. Help them to be released from fear's grip.

You must give birth to sons and daughters. Invite them to this brave life. It's no good to experience it alone. Isn't it better to do it with others?

WRITE IN THE SAND:

Do you have victory in your life that could benefit someone else? Are you mentoring someone right now? If yes, make sure you have a definitive plan of helping them to live the fearless life.

_____

_____

_____

_____

_____

_____

_____

GO FEARLESS

Pray about sharing your life with another lady. Everyone has something to offer someone. Become a mentor over the next 30 days.

Fearless Prayer

Father, In the name of Jesus,

I pray for humility and strength. Help me to see myself through your eyes and not my own. May I receive your love, bask in it and live from it. I pray that you would squash every point of fear in my life. Lavish your wisdom upon me so I may be ready to face any situation that arises. Lord, help me to walk in boldness and to do all that you have purposed in your heart that I would do for your kingdom. In Jesus's name, I pray. Amen.

ABOUT THE AUTHOR

Crystal Jones leads the FEARLESS Women's Conference that travels across the United States. She is the founder and director. She pastors and oversees several ministries with her husband. She has written several books including Unafraid. She has been joyfully living the adventurous life with the love of her life, Oscar Jones, for more than 35 years. They have 7 children (2 of which are in-laws) She has 8 grandchildren who have thoroughly blessed her life. She is a prophet, mentor, author, and conference speaker and lives in the Atlanta, Georgia area

Other Books by Crystal Jones

*I Want a Husband, Too!
*No Longer A Dream: A Step by Step Guide to Writing Your First Book
*Not Without My Daughters
*The S Word: What Submission Is Not
*Unafraid

Books Co-authored by Crystal Jones

*Church Unusual (Oscar Jones)
* Extreme Money Makeover (Oscar Jones)
*Fast Food for the Married Soul (Oscar Jones)
*Hot Dates for Married Lovers (Oscar Jones)
*Leadershift 3.0 (Oscar Jones)
*Let the Prophets Speak (Torrona Tillman)
*Naked Sex for Married Couples Only (Oscar Jones)
*Ring Talks (Oscar Jones)
*The Newlywed Handbook (Oscar Jones)
*When the Vow Breaks (Oscar Jones)

Anthologies by Crystal Jones

*A Woman's Place: Leading Ladies Speak
*Kid's Worship

www.ingramcontent.com/pod-product-compliance
Lightning Source LLC
Chambersburg PA
CBHW070459100426
42743CB00010B/1687